Step by Step

The Story of Corn

It Starts with a Seed

Robin Nelson

Lerner Publications ◆ Minneapolis

Lerner Publications Company
An imprint of Lerner Publishing Group, Inc.
241 First Avenue North
Minneapolis, MN 55401 USA

For reading levels and more information, look up this title at www.lernerbooks.com.

Image credits: BLOOMimage/Getty Images, p. 3; stevanovicigor/Getty Images, pp. 5, 23 (top right); fotokostic/Getty Images, pp. 7, 15; feellife/Getty Images, pp. 9, 13, 23 (lower right); Allexxandar/Getty Images, pp. 11, 23 (lower left); alexeys/Getty Images, p. 17, 23 (top left); Westend61/Getty Images, p. 19; Ann Schwede/Getty Images, p. 21; Inti St Clair/Getty Images, p. 22. Cover: artisteer/Getty Images (corn cob); threeseven/Getty Images (kernels).

Main body text set in Mikado a Medium.
Typeface provided by HVD Fonts.

Editor: Alison Lorenz **Designer:** Mary Ross **Photo Editor:** Cynthia Zemlicka

Library of Congress Cataloging-in-Publication Data

Names: Nelson, Robin, 1971- author.
Title: The story of corn : it starts with a seed / Robin Nelson.
Description: Minneapolis : Lerner Publications, 2021 | Series: Step by step | Includes bibliographical references and index. | Audience: Ages 4-8 | Audience: Grades K-1 | Summary: "A farmer plants a corn seed. What happens next? Readers watch a seed grow into a tall corn stalk with vivid photos and simple, sequential text"– Provided by publisher.
Identifiers: LCCN 2019045806 (print) | LCCN 2019045807 (ebook) | ISBN 9781541597747 (library binding) | ISBN 9781728401119 (ebook)
Subjects: LCSH: Corn—Juvenile literature.
Classification: LCC SB191.M2 N366 2021 (print) | LCC SB191.M2 (ebook) | DDC 633.1/5—dc23

LC record available at https://lccn.loc.gov/2019045806
LC ebook record available at https://lccn.loc.gov/2019045807

Manufactured in the United States of America
2-1008941-48365-9/28/2022

Corn tastes yummy.

How does it grow?

A farmer prepares for planting.

The farmer plants
seeds.

The seeds change.

Tiny plants grow.

Corn plants
grow tall.

The farmer protects
the plants.

Cobs grow.

Workers pick
the corn.

People buy
the corn.

Let's eat!

Picture Glossary

cobs

farmer

plants

seeds

Read More

Brannon, Cecelia H. *Corn*. New York: Enslow, 2018.

Roza, Greg. *My First Trip to a Farm*. New York: PowerKids, 2020.

Shea, Therese. *Harvesting Equipment*. New York: Enslow, 2020.

Index